GLADIATOR

Richard Watkins

Houghton Mifflin Company
Boston 1997

To Mom and Dad
Whose love, support, and typing skills
made this book possible.

For information about this and other Houghton Mifflin trade
and reference books and multimedia products, visit
The Bookstore at Houghton Mifflin on the World Wide Web
at http://www.hmco.com/trade/.

The text of this book is set in 14 point Baskerville Book.
The illustrations are marker, charcoal, and pencil.

Library of Congress Cataloging-in-Publication Data
Watkins, Richard Ross.
Gladiator / by Richard Watkins.
p. cm.
Summary: Describes the history of gladiators,
including types of armor, use of animals, amphitheaters, and how
the practice fit into Roman society for almost 700 years.
ISBN 0-395-82656-X
1. Gladiators — Rome — History — Juvenile literature.
[1. Gladiators. 2. Rome — History.] I. Title.
GV35.W38 1997
796.8 — dc20 96-21107 CIP AC

Manufactured in the United States of America
HOR 10 9 8 7 6 5 4 3 2 1

CONTENTS

INTRODUCTION

On a sunny afternoon two thousand years ago, the fiercest and strongest men in the Roman Empire marched out onto the sand of the arena. Fifty thousand spectators roared as these men, the gladiators, came into view, their magnificent armor glistening in the sun. When they came to a halt in front of the emperor's box, slaves came forward to present each with a razor-sharp weapon: sword, dagger, or spear. As the slaves scurried away the crowd fell silent. The gladiators raised their weapons to the emperor and called out, "Hail, Emperor! We who are about to die salute thee!" Trumpets blared, the men paired off, and with a clash of swords began the deadly combats of the gladiators of ancient Rome.

I

ANCIENT ROME

The gladiator's world was a Roman world. The civilization that developed and exploited them was the most powerful empire of its time. At its height, it governed the lives of 60 million people, one-fifth of the world's population, all of whom obeyed its laws, paid taxes to its emperor, and were familiar with its language, religions, and customs.

According to tradition, Rome was founded on April 21, 753 B.C. The legend says that Romulus and Remus were the twin sons of the war god, Mars. As infants, they were abandoned in a basket by the River Tiber. There they were found by a she-wolf, who carried them back to her den and protected and nurtured them until they were old enough to survive on their own. It was as a young man that Romulus established the city that bears his name by carving its borders with a plow. Watching his brother hard at work and doing nothing to help, Remus teased Romulus mercilessly, making fun of his hard labor. When he could take it no

2

longer, Romulus flew into a rage and attacked his twin, killing him. Romulus was not only the founder of Rome, but also its first king.

From this legendary beginning Rome grew to become the most important city in the western world. In 509 B.C. Rome's last king was dethroned and the Roman Republic was founded, ruled by two consuls who were elected each year by the senate. Military conquest and colonization brought the rest of Italy under Roman rule by 268 B.C. First to be absorbed were the Latins, Samnites, and other Italian tribes, followed by the great Etruscan civilization in the north and the Greek colonies in the south. The Romans adopted many elements of both the Etruscan and Greek cultures. Gladiator fights and chariot racing were Etruscan in origin. Roman art, architecture, and literature borrowed heavily from the Greeks.

Carthage, Rome's principal competition for trade in the Mediterranean Sea, was finally defeated in 146 B.C., after one hundred years of war. Further conquests followed: Gaul (what is now France) was conquered by Julius Caesar in 49 B.C., Egypt in 30 B.C., and Britain in A.D. 43.

All this expansion was not without a price. The democratic principles established by the Republic sank under the weight of the growing empire. Victorious generals fought for power in a series of bloody civil wars. Julius Caesar, after proclaiming himself permanent dictator, was murdered by a conspiracy of senators in 44 B.C. In the struggle for power that followed, Caesar's adopted son, Octavian, defeated all his political and military rivals and became Augustus Caesar, first emperor of Rome, in 27 B.C.

Augustus Caesar, Rome's first emperor

THE ROMAN EMPIRE

IN THE 2ND CENTURY A.D.

Until its fall four hundred years later, Rome was ruled by eighty-six emperors, some wise and just, others insane and corrupt. At its height, the Roman Empire controlled all of southern Europe, Britain, Asia Minor, Syria, Egypt, and North Africa. Cities were established, trade was regulated, taxes were collected. Rome built 53,000 miles of roads, bridges, aqueducts, and sewers, some of which are still in use. Its laws, manners, and customs were adopted all over the empire.

But for all its glory, it's difficult to ignore the fact that the Roman Empire was won by military force and built by the labor of millions of slaves. To the average Roman citizen, life was hard, war was a constant threat, and slaves were just another piece of property. And in spite of their sophistication in government, business, and the arts, Romans had a crude taste for violence and cruelty. For almost a thousand years Roman society represented both the best and the worst of human civilization.

II
THE FIRST GLADIATORS

The first known gladiatorial combat in Rome took place at the funeral of a nobleman named Junius Brutus in 264 B.C. His sons Marcus and Decimus revived an ancient Etruscan custom of having slaves fight at the funeral of a great leader in the belief that such a sacrifice would please the gods. During the ceremony, which took place in the Forum Boarium, or cattle market, three pairs of slaves were forced to fight to the death. This strange custom grew in popularity as more rich and powerful men presented these displays as part of the ceremonies to honor their dead.

In 216 B.C., twenty-two pairs of slaves fought at the funeral of a man named Marcus Lepidus. Sixty pairs fought when Publicus Licinius died in 183 B.C. These slave fighters were now known as *bustiarii*, funeral men. As Rome's taste for slave fights grew, so did the occasions that required them. If a family's reputation could be enhanced by these displays, then so could a politician's chance of election or a general's popu-

6

larity. It became clear that an ambitious Roman could buy a crowd's attention, ensure his social standing, and demonstrate his power over life and death.

By the time of Julius Caesar, any direct association with funerals and religion was gone, and these fighters, now known as *gladiators,* meaning swordsmen, were a powerful force in Roman politics. Caesar's genius at entertaining the masses with extravagant gladiatorial displays equaled his skills as a general and a politician. He bought the affection of the people with magnificent banquets and spectacles that were open and free to the public. He showered his political supporters and his *legionaries* (soldiers) with gold. All this gave Caesar unlimited power and established the precedent of keeping the populace occupied with triumphal processions, chariot races, and gladiator shows. The bigger the event, the more impressed the people were. In 46 B.C. Caesar staged a battle between two armies, each with 500 men, 30 cavalrymen, and 20 battle elephants. He topped that with a naval battle with 1,000 sailors and 2,000 oarsman, staged on a huge artificial lake dug just for that purpose.

These gladiatorial combats affirmed Julius Caesar's power and, to him, the cost in gold and human lives was worth it. Augustus Caesar, in 22 B.C., brought all games in Rome under his direct control, making them a state monopoly. He realized that the games were too important a political tool to be exploited by anyone else.

III
WHO WERE THE GLADIATORS?

Of the thousands of men who ended up in the arena, the vast majority were either prisoners of war, criminals, or slaves. As the Roman Empire grew through constant wars of conquest, soldiers of the defeated armies found themselves on the way to Rome, roped neck to neck with their arms tied behind their backs. Among them were Samnites, Thracians, and Gauls from territories conquered early in Rome's history, followed by Britons, Germans, Moors, and Africans, captives from virtually every land that became part of the empire. These human trains were whipped and beaten as they marched, or were packed into the dark and dirty holds of cargo ships bound for Rome. Captives ended up in Rome's slave markets to be auctioned off. Many of the biggest and strongest were bought for the gladiator schools to be trained for combat in the arena.

Criminals were another major source of gladiators. Originally, those convicted of murder, robbery, arson, or sacrilege were sent to the arena

to be killed by an executioner with a sword (*damnati ad gladium*) or thrown to the beasts (*damnati ad bestius*), in the belief that this would act as a deterrent for would-be criminals. As the games grew in popularity and entertainment became more important than deterrence, more criminals were sentenced to train in gladiator schools (*damnati in ludum*). The amount of instruction they received varied. In general, a sentence to the schools meant three years of training and combat in the arena followed by two years teaching in the schools (anyone who survived three years as a gladiator made an excellent teacher). Some of these convicted criminals turned gladiators learned their new profession well and became heroes of the arena, winning fame, fortune, and, possibly, freedom from further combat. Occasionally, though, large-scale shows demanded so many gladiators that any criminal, regardless of his crime, could find himself holding a sword and fighting for his life with little or no instruction whatsoever.

Ordinary slaves were the other major source of gladiators. Owners could dispose of their slaves any way they wanted, just like other property. A slave who tried to run away or was accused of theft or simply bored his master could be sent to the arena. It wasn't until the second century A.D. that owners were prohibited from sending a slave into the arena without just cause.

Obviously, prisoners of war, criminals, and slaves had no choice but to fight, so it is incredible to think that there were men who actually volunteered to be gladiators. At the height of the Roman Empire, more than half of all gladiators were in this deadly profession by their own

opposite page: Prisoners of war would often end up in Roman arenas fighting as gladiators.

choice. Most were simply poor and desperate, and the life of a gladiator, however short, offered regular meals and the dream of glory.

Champion gladiators who showed exceptional skill and bravery in the arena were sometimes presented with a wooden baton, the *rudius,* that awarded the champion honorable retirement from further combat. Many continued to fight, even after winning the *rudius,* knowing they could command a high price to enter the arena again, this time as a volunteer. The great Syrian gladiator Flamma (the Flame) earned four *rudi,* only to keep on fighting. The emperor Tiberius offered one thousand pieces of gold per performance to entice retired gladiators back to the arena. Many accepted, not only for the money, but to hear again the roar of the crowd and experience the thrill of combat.

Occasionally a nobleman would dare to be a gladiator. An appearance by one of these wealthy thrill-seekers would send the audience into a frenzy. To see an aristocrat fighting among the slaves and criminals thrilled the mob of *plebeians,* or common people, in the stands. The demand for them was so great at times that some emperors, Augustus and Tiberius in particular, tried to stop them, but there were always some noblemen ready to risk their lives in the arena. Sometimes, though, these privileged gladiators could fight without fearing for their lives. Their status would entitle them to special consideration, allowing them to fight not to the death, but only as a special exhibition between the regular fights. As popular as these blue-blooded gladiators were with the mob at the amphitheater, they were an embarrassment to their peers in the upper class.

The lure of the arena was so strong that even some emperors played at being gladiators, among them Caligula and Hadrian. The emperor Commodus did more than play. He claimed to have fought more than one thousand fights and paid himself one million *sesterces* for each. By comparison, a laborer in Rome might earn one thousand *sesterces* a year.

Because every level of Roman society had representatives in the arena, emperors and slaves, senators and criminals, it is not surprising that women also appeared as gladiators. They were considered a novelty, but a carving found in Halicarnassus in Asia Minor (what is now Turkey) shows a pair, one appropriately called Amazon, fighting with the same equipment and, apparently, the same intensity as men. The carving says they were honorably discharged. In one way, these women gladiators succeeded where men failed; they managed to offend Roman sensibilities enough to be banned in A.D. 200.

This tablet, found in Turkey, shows two women gladiators, Amazona and Achillia.

IV

THE SCHOOLS

It was no easy task to transform hordes of unwanted men into professional fighting machines. After all, many gladiators didn't volunteer. Men sold into slavery and dragged off to fight in the arena were not likely to be interested in putting on a good show for the Roman mob. It took brute force, lots of money, sophisticated training techniques, and an understanding of the human mind to get thousands of men to fight to the death and demonstrate not only power and skill but pride and dignity.

The development of the schools and the techniques used to produce the quality and quantity of professional gladiators followed the pattern of growth of the Roman Empire itself. Early in the history of gladiators, it was wealthy individuals who bought the men, trained them, and organized their combats. It wasn't long before men appeared who made their living by renting out their own troupes of gladiators — after reaching an agreement on the price to be paid for those gladiators killed or wounded. For an additional fee they would organize and produce a complete gladiator display, made to order. These businessmen were called *lanistae,* which comes from the Etruscan word for butcher. Romans considered this a dirty profession because they essentially were selling human lives. This attitude seems odd given the fact that buying gladiators and putting on a show was a sign of prestige and honor for a nobleman. Whatever the social status, the chance to make a profit encouraged the growth of the trade, and soon there were *lanistae* with their troupes of gladiators throughout the Roman Empire.

Even with troupes of gladiators crisscrossing every province, the demand still exceeded the supply. With the birth of the Roman Empire in 27 B.C. and its countless state holidays, official ceremonies, and special occasions decreed by the emperor, each requiring gladiatorial combat and animal fights, private contractors were unable to satisfy the enormous demands of the state. The numbers are staggering: 10,000 fought in the four-month-long series of games given by Trajan to celebrate the conquest of Dacia. In one year at the end of the second century A.D., Gordian I gave shows every month. At least 150 pairs of gladiators and sometimes up to 500 pairs fought at each display. These are just two examples of special shows given in Rome; add to that regular shows given on state holidays and all the shows given in every province of the empire. A well-organized network for procuring, training, and distributing these huge numbers of gladiators was needed.

The foundation for this network had existed for some time. The first gladiator schools were in Campania, a province some 100 miles south of Rome. Before the rise of Rome it had been a colony of the Etruscans,

15

who invented gladiator combat. It was from a school in Capua, which is in Campania, that Spartacus escaped in 73 B.C. to lead the greatest slave revolt in Roman history. What began as a gladiator school breakout of 70 men grew into an army of almost 90,000 escaped slaves that overran most of southern Italy. After two years the Roman army finally mustered enough strength to crush the rebellion. Spartacus was killed and the 6,000 rebels captured alive were crucified along the Via Appia, the main road leading to Rome. In spite of the fear Spartacus must have inspired in every Roman, the investment in private gladiator schools grew, as did the establishment of schools run by the state.

The private schools rented out gladiators for a set fee and received a standard price for any men killed. Imperial schools supplied gladiators exclusively for the emperor and for official state games. The size of the schools suggests how important they were in Roman culture. Julius Caesar owned a school in Capua that had enough armor for 5,000 gladiators. Rome had four large schools, all conveniently built near the Colosseum — the Great School (*Ludus Magnus*), the Gallic School (*Ludus Gallicus*), the Dacian School (*Ludus Dacius*), and the animal fighters school (*Ludus Matutinus*).

Gladiator schools were both prison camps and training centers. The techniques used to turn raw "recruits" into trained fighters were tough but effective. As soon as he was admitted to the school and passed a fitness test, a trainee found out what was expected of him when he took the gladiator's oath and swore, "I undertake to be burnt by fire, to be bound in chains, to be beaten by rods, and to die by the sword." He was made to believe he was joining a special group, and his survival de-

16

opposite page: A gladiator school instructor drills a group of tiros on swordsmanship.

pended on how well he learned his craft. Novices, or *tiros,* began their basic training with a wooden sword used against a straw man or a wooden post. The instructors were retired gladiators and they taught basic fencing skills, physical conditioning, and toughness. These veterans were critical to the development of quality gladiators. To the *tiros* these old-timers represented strength, skill, and, most important, survival. They told their students the stories of their great victories and taught them the tricks of the trade that might mean the difference between life and death.

When the novices mastered the basic skills, they began practicing against each other, first using simple wooden weapons, then iron weapons — heavy and blunt. These added strength without causing serious injury. When a student was considered ready, he would practice with real weapons to prepare for the experience of the arena.

There was an elaborate hierarchy in the schools. Within each discipline fighters ranged from first class (*primus palus* — gladiators with lots of combat experience) down to fourth class (new recruits with no experience). Living quarters were assigned according to these ranks. They also determined the fee paid to the school for the gladiator's services and the prize money he received for winning.

The high-ranking gladiators were expected not only to be leaders among their groups, but, more importantly, to introduce novices to the guild of the gladiators. The guild offered a sense of belonging and instilled loyalty in the men. It had its own myths and legends, its own god — Mars — and its own burial society, which provided an honorable funeral for its members, who were often refused burial in Roman cemeteries. The schools encouraged participation in the guild because it boosted morale and fostered the belief that the gladiators were members of an elite force. As a result, the schools could offer trained and loyal men to fight in the arena, ready to face death without fear.

V

TYPES OF GLADIATORS

This stone tablet shows an unknown type of gladiator with strange weapons strapped to each arm.

The earliest gladiators were outfitted in the equipment of the armies they conquered. As gladiator combats became more common, their weapons and armor became more specialized. These specialized forms evolved into six basic classifications of gladiators.

It is likely that the style of armor and weapons changed over time or varied somewhat from one part of the empire to another. There were also lesser-known types of gladiators who didn't fit into one of the basic gladiator categories. For example, the *lacquearius* tried to catch his opponent with a rope lasso, the *dimachaerus* fought with two swords, and the *eques* fought on horseback with a round shield and a lance. There are even a few types of gladiators that are completely unknown except for an image on a single carved stone tablet. But, over the long history of the Roman Empire, the basic categories of gladiators remained unchanged.

The illustrations on the following pages depict the types of gladiator most often mentioned in Roman writings and depicted in Roman artifacts.

SAMNITE

The first gladiator type, the Samnite is named after the people of Samnium, one of the earliest enemies of Rome. Samnites were heavily armored, wearing a visored helmet with a high crest decorated with feathers, and leather or metal bands around their arms and left legs. They carried a large, rectangular shield called a *scutum*. The straight sword they used was called a *gladius,* from which the word *gladiator* was derived.

HOPLOMACHUS

The *hoplomachus* was another heavily armored gladiator whose armor, weapon, and fighting style were very similar to those of the Samnite. In fact, archaeologists cannot confirm what differences, if any, there were between the two other than that until the reign of Augustus (31 B.C.–A.D. 14), all heavy gladiators were called Samnites, and after Augustus gladiators with heavy armor were called *hoplomachi*.

THRACIAN

The Thracian was lightly armored, carrying a very small round or square shield called a *parma* and a strange curved sword called a *sica*. His helmet had a large crest, sometimes in the shape of a griffin, a mythological beast. He wore leg guards on both legs, not just on the left leg, as did the Samnite and *hoplomachus*. These guards were very tall, covering the legs up to the tops of the thighs. The Thracian always fought against a heavily armored gladiator.

MIRMILLO

The *mirmillo,* or fish man, was identified by the images of fishes that decorated his helmet. He fought with a short sword and carried a large, round shield that helped to protect his unarmored legs. His name begins to make sense when one learns that he was often paired with the *retiarius,* who would try to catch his prey, the *mirmillo,* in his net. Even though he appears relatively unprotected, the *mirmillo,* along with the Samnite, *hoplomachus,* and *secutor,* was classified by the Romans as a "heavy" gladiator because of his large and heavy shield.

RETIARIUS

The *retiarius,* or net fighter, fought with a three-pronged fishing spear, called a *trident,* and a net. His fighting strategy was to entangle his opponent in his net and then skewer him as a fisherman would skewer his catch. Small lead weights around its edge helped spread the net when thrown, and with the attached cord the *retiarius* could draw it back if he missed his opponent. Unlike other gladiators, the *retiarius* wore almost no armor. He wore only a headband — no helmet — and his sole protection was a guard on his left arm with a large flat shoulder piece.

SECUTOR

The *secutor*, or chaser, got his name from his fighting technique, which was to chase his opponent around the arena. He wore a round, crested helmet with two small, round eye holes. The rounded shape was less likely to become entangled in the net of the *retiarius*, or net fighter, his principal opponent. His right arm was covered with protective leather or metal bands, and in his right hand he carried a short sword or dagger. With his left hand he carried a large shield, and on his left leg he wore a metal leg guard, called an *ocrea*, so his left side was completely protected.

VI
ANIMALS IN THE ARENA

Displays of exotic animals were seen in every ancient civilization. Strange and ferocious animals captured in faraway lands were the perfect symbol of a ruler's power. The royalty of China and Egypt showed off collections of animals to visiting dignitaries a thousand years before the rise of Rome. Alexander the Great collected animals from every part of his vast empire. The Romans, however, weren't content with passive displays of wild animals, and they added the ingredient that was the hallmark of all their public spectacles — bloodshed. They liked to watch animals fight each other to the death. They liked to watch men hunt down and kill wild animals. They also liked to watch wild animals hunt down and kill men, and sometimes women and children.

These bloody shows, called *venationes,* began the same way the gladiator fights did, as religious ceremonies. The ancient festival given in honor of Flora, goddess of flowers, was celebrated with a public hunt of goats and hares. During the festival of Ceres, goddess of agriculture, foxes were set loose in the Circus Maximus, the chariot racing stadium, with torches tied to their tails. Animal welfare apparently was not an issue in ancient Rome.

Venationes became more and more popular, and by the second century B.C. they were part of nearly every public celebration. Giving a *venatio* became popular with the rich and powerful as a way to show off. Every effort was made to surpass the previous shows in cost and splendor. Strange creatures, never seen before, were introduced to the arena. Lions and leopards appeared in Rome for the first time in the third century B.C. Romans had seen their first elephant in the triumphal procession given by Curius in 275 B.C., eleven years before the first gladiator show. Soon gladiators and animals appeared regularly in the same celebration, but always as a separate event.

During the empire, most *ludi,* or games, followed a standard format: *venationes* in the morning and *munera* (gladiator fights) in the afternoon. By this time, animal shows were a state-run business. The imperial government alone had the money, influence, and manpower to supply the huge numbers of animals required for their great spectacles. Hundreds, even thousands of animals might be used in the arena in one day. In fact, five thousand animals appeared in a single display during the games that opened the Colosseum in A.D. 80. And, since the Romans showed no interest in breeding captive animals, those animals killed in each event had to be replaced with others shipped from their native lands in time for the next *venatio*. The Roman state used three methods to find animals: they were bought from agents throughout the empire who specialized in the trapping and trading of wild animals; the emperor could ask a provincial governor to supply them, which the governor promptly did if he wanted to keep his job; or they were acquired through military conquest — victorious generals always brought back exotic creatures among their spoils of war to be used in the games given to celebrate their triumph.

A *venatio* usually featured several kinds of events, often beginning with animals trained to perform amazing tricks. Small boys would dance on the backs of wild bulls; lions would catch hares in their teeth and return them unharmed to their masters. Teams of panthers pulled chariots around the arena, and tigers licked the hands of the trainers who had whipped them only moments before. Elephants, whose appearance was always a highlight in the shows, walked on a tightrope or danced to the sound of cymbals played by other elephants; one in particular was trained to kneel before the imperial box and write witty remarks in the sand with its trunk. These displays of the animal trainer's talents were only a warm-up to the acts the crowd really wanted to see, events designed to kill as many animals and people as possible.

Animal shows featured the slaughter of large numbers of animals by specially trained men, called *bestiarii*. They wore only a simple linen tunic, not the extravagant armor of the gladiators, and typically carried a single long-bladed spear, the *venabulum*. Other animal fighters, armed with either bow and arrows *(sagittarii)* or a sword and shield, were not uncommon. Most were slaves, although a few did volunteer and, like the gladiators, learned their skills in their own imperial training school. They took pride in their work and wore the scars inflicted by the teeth and claws of their opponents like badges of courage. To prove their

bravery, some *bestiarii* would stun a wild bear with punches from their bare fists, then kill it with their spear. Others would wait for a lion to charge, then toss their cape over its head, blinding it before they finished it off. The *bestiarius* who first waved a red cape in the face of a maddened bull began the tradition of the matador, an ancient craft still practiced at the bullfights of Mexico and Spain. It was a dangerous job, and few survived for long. Like the gladiators, animal fighters were considered social outcasts. But even the gladiators looked down on the *bestiarii*. Maybe it was because they only fought animals, whereas the gladiators fought other armed men. For whatever reason, there is no record of any *bestiarius* rising above his low status, as some champion gladiators did.

Another feature of the games was watching animals fight each other. Rhinoceroses fought elephants, their horns and tusks sheathed with sharp iron spikes. Elephants fought *aurochs*, huge wild bison, now extinct, due in part to their popularity in the arena. Bison fought bear; bear fought lion. Any combination that would bring about violence and death, even if the combatants had to be prodded with spears or torches.

After scenes where so many animals were destroyed, the animals were given a chance to be the destroyers. Criminals, runaway slaves, Jews or Christians, anyone condemned as an undesirable, was torn apart by leopards, lions, or bears. Gladiators and animal fighters had a chance, however slim, of survival; condemnation to the beasts meant certain death. Of the many thousands of people sentenced to be killed by wild animals, only one, a young man named Androcles, left the arena alive.

opposite page: A venatio often included a display of amazing animal tricks.

The beast released into the arena to kill Androcles was a huge lion that bounded toward his victim, but instead of attacking, laid down and licked his feet. The emperor Caligula, utterly amazed by this scene, demanded an explanation from the young man. Androcles, a runaway slave, told the emperor that he had hidden in a cave after his escape and inside had come upon a lion crippled by a thorn embedded deep in his paw. Androcles removed the thorn and for the next three years the grateful lion acted like his faithful servant. Androcles was eventually recaptured and the lion, trapped soon afterward, was by chance shipped off to appear in the same arena as Androcles.

Even though it is hard to see how any good could have come from such waste of animal and human life, there was one result of the *venationes* that may be considered positive. Many new lands were opened up to colonization and farming after they were cleared of the dangerous predators that were trapped in order to maintain a steady supply of animals for the empire's amphitheaters.

VII
THE AMPHITHEATER

The earliest gladiators fought wherever there was room enough for both the combatants and the spectators. From the first gladiator fight, which was held in Rome's cattle market, until the end of the first century B.C., gladiator combats continued to be given in the various forums around the city, principally the Forum Romanum. Temporary wooden stands were erected and then dismantled as soon as the fights were over.

The chariot racing stadium, or Circus Maximus, was also the setting for gladiator shows, but it proved to be less than ideal for watching hand-to-hand combat. There were plenty of seats, more than 100,000, but they were spread over a 2,000-foot-long track with a *spina* (spine or divider) running down the middle, so few spectators had a good view of a duel.

The type of building best suited for viewing gladiator combats and animal shows was the amphitheater, which was oval in shape with a central fighting area surrounded by concentric rows of seats. The word *amphitheater* is Greek, meaning a theater with seats on all sides. The central fighting area was called the *arena*, which is the Latin word for sand. Sand was the ideal covering for the floor of the amphitheater because it soaked up the blood, and was easily raked over or replaced. For a change of pace the emperor Claudius once had borax, which is a pure white mineral, spread on the arena floor, and Nero used cinnabar, a mineral that is bright red.

The oldest existing ruins of an amphitheater are in Pompeii, in the region of Campania in Italy. It was here that gladiator combat probably developed from its earliest roots. Built around 80 B.C., the amphitheater could hold almost 20,000 people, half the town's population.

The Romans recognized the need for sturdy and permanent structures for their games and eventually built hundreds of amphitheaters throughout the empire. Gladiators continued to fight in forums and markets, but amphitheaters, with their sweeping curves and arches, became the true monuments of the games.

The most magnificent amphitheater of all is the Amphitheatrum Flavium (Flavian Amphitheater) in Rome, which was officially named after the emperor who ordered its construction in A.D. 74, Titus Flavius Sabinus Vespasianus, known as Vespasian. He didn't live to see his dream project completed, but his son, the emperor Titus, ordered work to continue and spared no expense in the amphitheater's construction. Smooth white plaster covered the rough exterior stonework. The ceilings of the seventy-two interior staircases were painted gold and purple and all the inside walls were faced with marble. Titus opened the great amphitheater in A.D. 80 with one hundred consecutive days of animal hunts and gladiator shows.

No one can say how it got its more popular name, the Colosseum, but the simplest explanation is that the name was given to the building centuries later because of its "colossal" size. The outside dimensions are 613 feet by 508 feet, and the arena itself measures 282 feet by 177 feet — about the same as a modern football field, which is 300 feet by 150 feet. The Colosseum could seat 45,000 spectators on its marble benches, and another 5,000 could stand on the top tier. The seating areas were divided according to social class, with the best seats closest to the arena. These belonged to the emperor, senators, priests and priestesses, foreign kings, and ambassadors. Above this first level, called the *podium,* sat the *patricians,* or noblemen, and above that ordinary Roman citizens. The highest tier was left to foreigners, the poor, and slaves.

At the very top edge of the outside wall were 240 tall wooden masts that supported a vast canvas awning, the *velarium,* which could shade the entire amphitheater. Rigged with an intricate system of ropes and pulleys, a specially trained squadron of sailors (used because they were already experts with sails and rigging) could position the awning to cover or uncover any part of the stands at the emperor's command. If they displeased their ruler, rowdy spectators could find themselves open to the scorching Roman sun while the rest of the stands were covered by a cooling shade.

Another feature of this enormous structure emphasized its terrible purpose. Underneath the floor of the arena was a complex network of

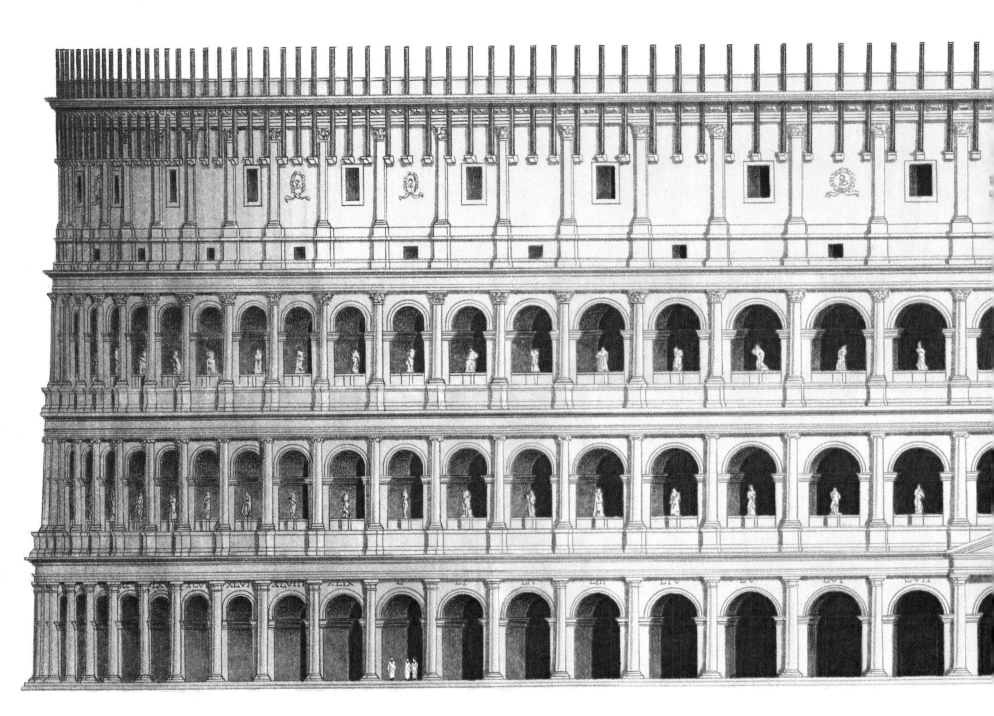

Exterior of the Colosseum

Cut-away view of the interior of the Colosseum

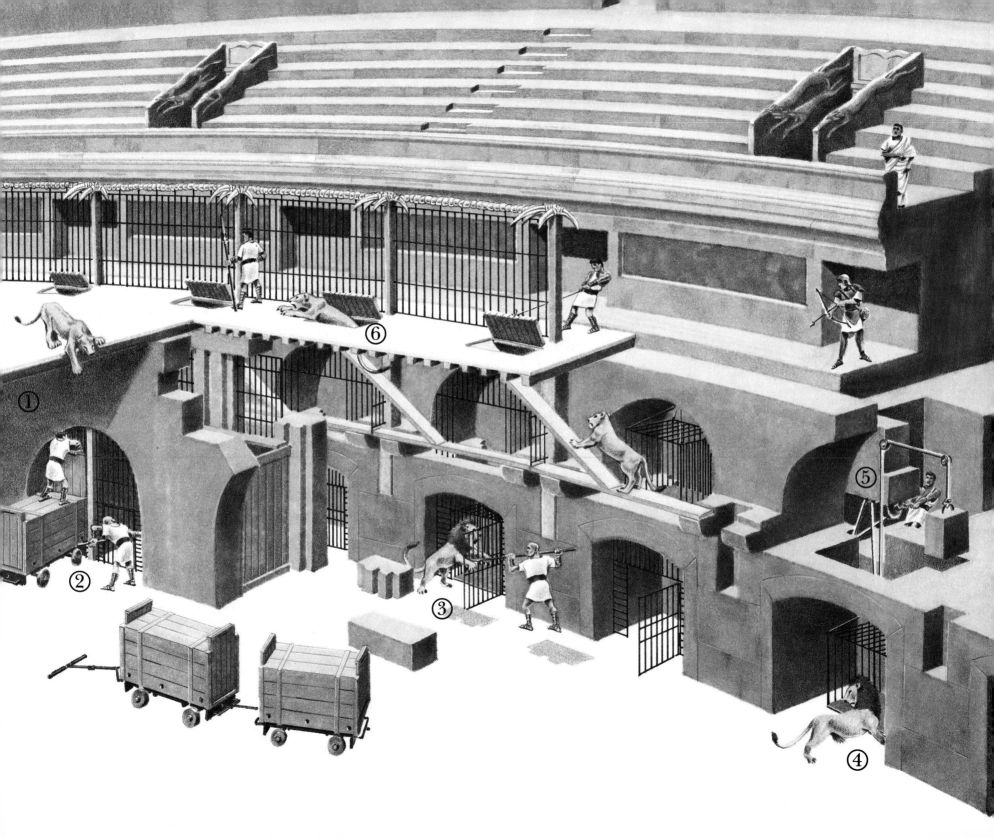

chambers and tunnels built late in the second century A.D. to accommodate a variety of special effects. During the games, animals and props would magically rise from under the arena. Whole sections of the floor could be lowered, set with elaborate props or scenery, then raised to provide an extravagant backdrop for the hunts. Many lions could be lifted simultaneously in thirty-two elevators at the perimeter of the arena floor. In these manmade caverns were an armory, a first-aid station, and a morgue to receive the dead. There was also a system of tunnels that led out under the city to warehouses, holding cages for animals, and to the gladiator training schools. The manpower required to operate shows on such a large scale must have been in the hundreds, or even thousands.

The paint and marble are long gone, but the Colosseum, a symbol of Rome's power, still stands after almost two thousand years as one of the world's greatest architectural achievements. But it is also a symbol of Rome's cruelty — an engineering masterpiece devoted solely to the slaughter of men and animals for the pleasure of the crowd.

opposite page: Animals were released
into the arena from thirty-two elevators
under the arena floor:

1. Lions are released into holding cells.
2. Arena slaves prod lion into narrow passage.
3. Lion follows passage to elevator cage.
4. Lion enters cage.
5. Slave releases counterweight to raise elevator.
6. Lion jumps out of cage, runs up ramp and
   through trap door in floor of arena.

VIII
THE SEA BATTLES

The biggest gladiatorial combats in the history of the Roman Empire took place on water. Manmade lakes were dug specifically to stage full-scale naval battles. In the quest to provide the most spectacular games imaginable, some emperors outgrew even the biggest amphitheater. Julius Caesar presented the first recorded *naumachia* (sea fight) on a specially excavated lake in 46 B.C. It was fitting that Caesar should be the first, since it was he who contributed so much to the practice of producing massive spectacles to win public favor. He recreated a battle with 1,000 sailors and 2,000 oarsmen, outfitted in the arms and armor of the navies of Egypt and the ancient city of Tyre. Tens of thousands of spectators crowded the banks of the lake to witness the event. Many had camped for days along the roads leading to the site.

In 2 B.C. Augustus staged a naval battle to honor Julius Caesar and, of course, to outdo him. The lake dug next to the Tiber River was 1,800 feet long, 1,200 feet across, and was surrounded by parks and gardens.

It even had a manmade island in the middle. Six thousand gladiators and an even greater number of oarsmen, outfitted as Athenians and Persians, rowed into battle aboard thirty *biremes* (galleys with two banks of oars) and *triremes* (galleys with three banks of oars) equipped with iron battering rams.

Some sea battles were staged in the amphitheater, the arena flooded for the occasion. Nero released sharks and other dangerous sea creatures into the water-filled arena before his *naumachia,* no doubt to make it more realistic. The battle was real enough to the gladiators, who probably didn't enjoy the thought of hungry fish waiting for them if they fell into the water.

When Titus opened the Colosseum in A.D. 80 with one hundred days of games, he included a naval battle along with the more typical gladiator fights, animal shows, and chariot races. The Colosseum was built with huge cisterns and drainage pipes to allow Titus to flood the arena and board it over for the opening day of gladiators and animals. On the second day, chariots raced over the sand-covered boards. On the third day, the sand and boards were removed and a naval battle was fought between gladiators uniformed as soldiers from the Greek cities of Athens and Syracuse. The Athenian gladiators won and then staged an assault on a fortress built on a small island in the center of the arena.

One hundred years later, when the underground passages and machinery were built for the increasingly complex gladiator and animal shows, the arena could no longer be flooded. Sea battles had to be held elsewhere at specially constructed sites.

The most spectacular *naumachia* of all was given by the emperor Clau-

pp. 42–43: The Colosseum could be flooded for a naumachia.

The emperor Claudius gave the largest naumachia in Roman history.

dius in A.D. 52. To celebrate the completion of the tunnel between the Fucine Lake and the Liris River, Claudius amassed 19,000 gladiators on *triremes* and *quadriremes* (three- and four-decked galleys) to reenact a battle between the navies of the islands of Rhodes and Sicily. Surrounding the fleets, but leaving plenty of room to maneuver, was a ring of rafts manned by the Praetorian Guard (the emperor's elite army). On the shore of the lake, Claudius built ramparts on which he stationed more soldiers and catapults to discourage any thoughts of escape. Thousands of spectators watched from the sloping banks of the lake, which formed a natural amphitheater. A silver statue of Triton (son of Neptune, god of the sea) rose out of the lake and sounded his conch-shell trumpet, signaling the battle to begin. Hundreds of war galleys skillfully rowed, steered, and rammed each other. Sometimes they drew close enough to send boarding parties across to the enemy ships. This was no small reenactment — this was real naval warfare, produced to inflate Claudius's ego.

According to records, this otherwise rational emperor almost ruined his own show before it even started. Dressed in full military uniform, Claudius listened as the 19,000 warriors shouted out the traditional oath to their emperor. Claudius then cracked a bad joke, which either offended the gladiators or made them think they didn't have to fight. Either way, they all refused to start the battle. Claudius threatened to destroy the fleet and all those on board with his soldiers and catapults. The gladiators still refused. Claudius realized that a massacre of 19,000 men was not the kind of spectacle he wanted to be remembered for, so he went to the water's edge and pleaded with them to fight. Apparently

44

he was convincing, for the battle began and was fought bravely. Many were killed and wounded, but the lives of the survivors were spared.

Only a few emperors went to the trouble of providing sea battles for public entertainment. The site had to be dug or the amphitheater engineered so it would hold water, ships had to be built, and gladiators and oarsmen trained. Months, and possibly years, of preparation were required for one sea fight. A *naumachia* was on a scale even bigger than the usual massive Roman games, and, for the average Roman citizen, it was a once-in-a-lifetime experience to see one.

IX
THE GLADIATOR IN SOCIETY

Gladiators belonged to the lowest class of Roman society, and within that class they held the lowest rank. Their only function was to provide a few moments of entertainment, and whether they lived or died was not considered important. Gladiators carried their shameful reputation with them even after death; an inscription at a Roman cemetery lists the three classes of people who were forbidden burial: suicides, prostitutes, and gladiators.

But for an occupation that was so disgraceful, gladiators occupied a surprisingly important part in everyday life. Roman households might have evidence of the gladiators' popularity — a terra cotta oil lamp in the shape of a Thracian gladiator or a porcelain vase decorated with scenes of the arena. The homes of the wealthy often had intricate mosaics depicting gladiator fights in graphic detail.

Gladiators were such a significant part of Roman popular culture that an entire set of superstitions grew around them. Souvenirs from dead

opposite page:

top left: Ivory knife handle
top right: Clay pot
center: Bronze statue of a retiarius
bottom left: Small bronze figurine of a Thracian gladiator
bottom right: Terra cotta oil lamp in the shape of a gladiator helmet

gladiators were always in great demand. A piece of their clothing would ward off evil spirits. The blood of gladiators was used in certain magic potions and medicinal ointments. A bride who parted her hair with a dead gladiator's spear would have a happy marriage.

Gladiators as individuals were invisible until they did something special — until they not just won, but won with style. Popular gladiators made great efforts to develop an image that would attract attention in the arena. The shining armor and huge plumes of feathers on their ornate helmets were one aspect, but a flashy fighting style, a colorful name — such as Rodan or Hercules — and a flamboyant personality enhanced a gladiator's reputation both in and out of the arena. This wasn't just to show off, but rather for a deadly serious reason: if a gladiator should lose and find himself at the mercy of the crowd, they might let him live if he was fun to watch or if he had created a popular image. A boring gladiator was a dead gladiator.

A winning gladiator could almost become a worthwhile human being in the eyes of the Roman upper classes. People began to recognize him in the streets after his portrait was painted on walls throughout the city. Tavern keepers provided free food and drink, and girls would pursue him and compete for his attention. As his reputation grew, he became more and more like a rock star or sports hero is today.

If a celebrity gladiator continued to win, he might become a wealthy man, and maybe even retire to live a long and happy life. It didn't happen often. For every Spiculus — a *mirmillo* who won a palace from the emperor Nero — there were a thousand champion gladiators who never got to enjoy their prizes. Their winning streak would end, and so

opposite page: Popular gladiators were given free food and drink by tavern owners.

would their lives. And for every one thousand champion gladiators there were ten thousand losers, whose only taste of fame and fortune was in their dreams.

In spite of the risks of this most dangerous profession, some gladiators lived, or tried to live, normal lives with their wives and children. A slave gladiator would try to win his freedom and then buy freedom for his family. A freedman (an ex-slave) or a volunteer gladiator would try to win enough prize money to make his family's life better.

The attitudes of the emperors toward the games were as varied as the personalities of the emperors themselves. Augustus was smart enough to take control of the games, recognizing their political importance. Caligula, Claudius, and Nero all loved the cruelty and bloodshed of the arena and went to extremes, even by Roman tastes, to make the shows more exciting. Nero forced handicapped people to fight, and Caligula once ordered a whole section of spectators thrown to the beasts when he thought they laughed at him. This was, no doubt, the worst example of audience participation in history. Claudius would arrive at the arena before dawn, alone if necessary, so he wouldn't miss one minute of his own terrible spectacles.

Other emperors, Tiberius for example, were bored with the games and attended only because it was considered the emperor's duty to preside at his own show. Marcus Aurelius, who ruled from A.D. 161–180, tried unsuccessfully to reduce the number of holidays set aside for public entertainment. By that time, up to 193 days of the year were set aside for festivals, chariot races, gladiator battles, or animal fights.

Regardless of their feelings about the games, every emperor, and every Roman for that matter, recognized gladiators as a potential danger. They were, after all, professional killers.

Ever since the revolt of Spartacus, Rome realized that men forced to risk their lives in the arena would be desperate enough to fight and kill for their freedom. Rome learned to guard carefully against any more slave uprisings. Most gladiators were confined to the schools and were always disarmed after each practice or performance. Soldiers were posted at all the schools to prevent breakouts. Only first-rate gladiators — those who had earned special privileges due to their performance in the arena — were allowed leave to roam the city. Rebellions continued to occur, but none was as widespread or as threatening as the one led by Spartacus.

In spite of the obvious danger gladiators posed to individuals and to society in general, Rome came to depend on them. The people expected their bloody games, and the emperors would never risk disappointing their subjects. It became a vicious cycle: the mob demanded more and more extravagant shows, and the emperor would spare no expense to meet, and hopefully exceed, their expectations, thereby satisfying the mob and his ego at the same time.

Why were gladiators such an important part of Roman society? Why were a people who were, by all accounts, staid and conservative as individuals transformed into a bloodthirsty mob when packed together in the amphitheater? There were several reasons. For one, Rome was a warlike society. Glory in war was a Roman virtue, and by witnessing warlike scenes the people were supposed to become better prepared for the real thing. Another reason gladiators were so popular was that they appealed to the lower instincts of the mob. Spectators crowded together in the stands lost their sense of individuality and did not feel responsible for their actions. They could release their violent urges by watching scenes of cruelty; they could safely witness the thing they most feared — violent death — and be comforted in the knowledge that they, unlike the losing gladiators, would walk out of the amphitheater alive.

Probably the greatest reason the gladiators became such an important element of society is that the Romans had no concept of human rights. Public execution, persecution of any group that failed to declare their obedience to the emperor, and slavery were taken for granted. Everyone — emperor, senator, priest, teacher, and slave alike — accepted these things as the natural order. Ancient Rome wasn't the only culture to have such attitudes. Every civilization in the ancient world, and even some in our modern world, had or still have cruel and inhumane practices. Rome, however, surpassed all other cultures, ancient or modern, in its reliance on slavery. At the height of the empire virtually all unskilled labor was done by slaves. Not only were farming, mining, manufacturing, and construction all performed by slave labor, but the overseers, accountants, engineers, and architects were most likely slaves or freed slaves themselves.

At times in Rome's history, there were more slaves or freedmen in the city than there were free-born citizens. Since slaves could be bought much cheaper than the cost of paying a free man, large numbers of Romans were left unemployed. Spending great amounts of money and resources to provide free food and entertainment for the unemployed mob was the price Rome had to pay for its dependence on slavery. Rome refused to recognize the importance of these enslaved human beings. While some were treated well, most suffered at the hands of their masters. They could be bought, sold, beaten, whipped, and, until the second century A.D., killed by their owners for any reason; after A.D. 200, owners had to have a justifiable reason for the execution of a slave.

It was this kind of environment that created the gladiators. A culture that accepted the idea that certain human beings were nothing more than disposable property could easily watch them fight to the death.

X

A DAY AT THE GAMES

In the predawn hours the streets of Rome were usually dark and quiet, but on the day of an imperial show the streets and plazas surrounding the Colosseum were bustling with activity. Merchants of all types completely surrounded the amphitheater with awnings and stalls. They knew they could expect a huge crowd because the day's show had been heavily promoted for weeks. Billboards that announced the special events and star performers were painted on the sides of buildings all over the city. By sunrise the merchants were busy selling their wares as the crowd streamed into the Colosseum. Along with food and wine, people bought programs and placed bets on their favorite gladiators with bookmakers. Soon every seat was filled, and the crowd anxiously awaited the start of the show.

The sound of trumpets focused the crowd's attention to the entrance gate at one end of the arena. Romans loved lavish parades, and no imperial show would be complete if it didn't begin with one. The procession was led by twelve *lictors,* the traditional bodyguards of the consuls during the old republic. Each carried the *fasces,* an ax surrounded by a bundle of rods, the premier symbol of the Roman government. This wasn't just a customary display, but a reminder to the audience that everything they saw, the animals, the gladiators, even the building they were sitting in, was provided for their entertainment by their benevolent leader, the emperor. After the *lictors* came musicians, dancers, and a display of tamed exotic animals — row after row of leopards in silver harnesses, stags trained to pull a gilded chariot, bulls painted white and draped with fresh-cut flowers.

After this lighthearted beginning, the procession turned more serious as priests appeared carrying tall staffs topped with burning incense. More priests followed, leading sacrificial animals — rams, bulls, and hogs. Statues of all the gods (the Romans had dozens of them — gods, demigods, muses, graces, and emperors turned into gods), each borne on a litter by eight uniformed slaves, slowly moved around the arena. With another trumpet blast, the crowd came to its feet for the entrance of the royal family. Escorted by the imperial guards with their flowing scarlet capes and shining helmets, the royal family entered the amphitheater through a tunnel that led from the emperor's private entrance straight to the imperial box. After the various family members took their seats and the guards assumed their positions behind the marble throne set in the center of the box, the Colosseum fell silent. Every person in the stands rose to his feet. After an appropriately dramatic pause, in stepped the emperor of Rome, Septimus Severus. The crowd went crazy. He stood before his throne and waved regally to the people and then,

with a slight nod of his head, the games began.

One hundred ostriches and one hundred stags were released into the arena. The hunt was on. Twenty archers rushed onto the sand from each end of the amphitheater. They calmly chose their targets and drew their bows. Arrows whistled through the air. The animals scattered in all directions, but there was no escape. One after another they fell, and within minutes this first act of the *venatio* was over. Slaves rushed in with hooks and ropes to drag away the carcasses.

Before the audience could catch its breath, the floor of the arena opened up, and out of the depths rose a huge wooden ship. It had barely reached the arena level when it suddenly broke apart, letting loose hundreds of animals: lions, bears, leopards, and aurochs. Chaos erupted amid the ruins of the ship. Fifty *bestiarii* charged into the arena and met any beast who attacked them with the point of their long spears. One after another the animals fell — an ox was pulled down by three lions, a bear was skewered by a *bestiarius*. Many animal fighters died, too. One was pounced on from behind by a leopard; another was trampled by an ox. Twenty men were left unscathed after the last creature was killed. They gathered in the center of the arena to raise their spears in triumph and acknowledge the crowd, but their ordeal was not over. Around the edge of the arena, thirty-two trap doors sprang open in a cloud of sand. Out of each charged a large, muscular lion with a full, dark mane. In the bloody battle that followed, many more men and beasts were killed, and when the dust settled only six *bestiarii* were left alive to fight another day. The crowd broke into a chorus of cheers for the emperor to thank him for such a spectacular display.

57

Severus acknowledged his subjects with another wave of his hand and, when he did, two slaves appeared at each entrance throughout the amphitheater. One held a basket filled wooden balls (*missilia*), each marked with a different number. The other slave in each team tossed the balls into the seats, creating a free-for-all as spectators tried to grab one, because each could be redeemed for a prize after the show. While some of the prizes were modest — meat, flour, or livestock — others were worth scrambling for — money, slaves, even houses and land. A small army of slaves was busy in the arena while the crowd was distracted. The bodies of men and animals were dragged away, the wreckage of the ship was loaded onto wagons, and fresh sand was spread.

It was now close to noon and the bright sun was beating down on the spectators, packed together and wearing their heavy wool togas. They needed some relief. At the emperor's command, fountains rose around the perimeter of the arena and began to spray a cool mist of perfumed water that was carried through the crowd by the breeze. One hundred and fifty feet above the floor of the amphitheater, the special team of sailors scrambled over a network of ropes. They unrolled long strips of canvas that soon formed a huge awning that provided shade for the audience but left an elliptical opening directly over the arena.

While the crowd appreciated the emperor's efforts to make them comfortable, several hundred men were driven into the arena. They were called *gladiatores meridiani,* which means midday fighters, because of the time of day they were usually forced to perform. However, they weren't trained gladiators at all, just common criminals, runaway slaves, and other assorted social outcasts. Two men were chosen; one was given a

59

sword and ordered at spearpoint to kill the other, who was unarmed. His ugly job complete, he was disarmed and killed by the next man. This vicious cycle of butchery continued until the last man was struck down by an arena guard. As the last body was removed, in came another group of victims, men and women of all ages, each one tied to a post standing on a small, wheeled cart. Slaves pushed these carts in and around the arena to the jeers of the crowd, then formed a circle in the center with the captives facing the stands. With a loud clap the trap doors snapped open again and out flew one hundred leopards, all specially trained to attack humans. The slaves were careful to keep the carts between themselves and the leopards to avoid becoming victims, too. The dreadful screams of the poor souls on the carts were drowned out by cruel jokes and mocking cries from the stands until finally it was over, the carts were rolled out, and the leopards driven back to their cages under the arena. This disgusting display was merely a diversion during the noontime intermission. It was the Roman version of the halftime shows seen at our football games. Many in the audience may have left the stadium to get something to eat from the venders outside, or lounged in their seats, flirting and gossiping, oblivious to the suffering in the sand.

The intermission over, everyone returned to their seats to wait for the entrance of the stars of the show; the gladiators. But first there would be a whole afternoon of preliminary bouts and special displays before the big-name fights began.

The first act of the afternoon was a series of mock fights with wooden weapons. The *paegniarii,* one type of mock fighter, were armed with a whip in one hand and a club in the other. Brutal as this seems to us, these nonlethal fights were nothing but a tame warm-up act.

The distinctive sound of Roman war trumpets, or *tubae,* signaled the entrance of one hundred gladiators — fifty *hoplomachi* and fifty Thracians — in magnificent armor, each wearing a beautiful cape embroidered in gold. Valets marched alongside carrying their weapons. The troop came to a halt in front of the imperial box and shouted out, "Hail, Emperor! We who are about to die salute thee!" Severus nodded solemnly, and several of the officials who organized these games on behalf of their emperor came down from the box to the arena floor to inspect the weapons. If they were determined to be razor-sharp and were approved by the emperor, they were then distributed, and the gladiators spread out around the arena and paired off. Each man's opponent was drawn by lot before they entered the arena. With another nod of his head, Severus ordered the combat to begin.

The clash of sword against shield was soon accompanied by the sound of a band playing lively music from a stage set against the arena wall. Horns, flutes, and even a hydraulic organ could be heard as the gladiators fought for their lives. The crowd shouted encouragement to whichever type of fighter they favored, "lights" or "heavies" (Thracians or *hoplomachi*), and cursed any fighter who failed to show spirit.

In a flash a gladiator went down, a *hoplomachus* clutching a deep wound in his side inflicted by the wicked, curved sword of his Thracian opponent. The *hoplomachus* raised the first finger of his left hand — the tradi-

61

pp. 62–63: Fifty Thracians battle fifty hoplomachi.

tional sign for mercy. Officially it was up to the *editor,* the giver of the games, to decide the fallen gladiator's fate; in reality, the *editor,* in this case the emperor, usually followed the wishes of the crowd. If the gladiator had fought bravely, the crowd would respond by waving their handkerchiefs, raising their thumbs, and shouting, *"Mitte!"* ("Let him go!") The emperor would then raise his thumb and the loser would be allowed to leave the arena alive (called *missus*) through the Porta Sanavivaria, the Gate of Life.

Roman audiences weren't known for their compassion, so it took an extraordinary display of bravery for a loser to be granted a *missus.* This *hoplomachus* had fought well, but not well enough, and was therefore doomed. The crowd shouted, *"Iugula!"* ("Kill him!") and the emperor, with his arm outstretched, turned his thumb down (*pollice verso*). Accepting his fate without a whimper, the vanquished gladiator, still holding his side as he knelt in the sand, calmly turned his head, offering his bare neck to his conqueror. The Thracian bowed to the emperor, raised his sword, and in an instant left the *hoplomachus* crumpled at his feet. The spectators, getting their first taste of gladiator's blood, roared their approval. Into the arena rushed a team of slave attendants. One appeared as the Etruscan demon of death, Charun, wearing a horrible mask with horns and dressed entirely in black. He carried a huge hammer, which he used to make sure the loser was really dead. The others were dressed as the god Mercury in winged helmets and white tunics. According to Roman mythology, Mercury led the souls of the dead to the underworld. In a cruel parody of the myth, these slaves dragged the dead gladiator away through the *Porta Libitinensis,* the Gate of Death, named after the goddess of death, Libitina.

The *hoplomachus* was forgotten as soon as his body disappeared through the gate. The victorious Thracian could now celebrate his success while the forty-nine other duels were slashing and crashing their way to their fatal conclusions. He strutted proudly to the imperial box and was awarded the traditional symbol of victory, a palm branch, along with a modest cash prize. This was the greatest moment in his life; he had not only survived but won and, for a moment at least, was a hero to the Roman public. Dreams of glory must have danced in his head. Maybe he would win again tomorrow, and even win his freedom from the arena, with enough money to live an easy life in the country. But with those dreams came the chilling thought that he could just as easily wind up at the end of an iron hook, being dragged through the Gate of Death. His few moments as the center of attention over, he was escorted out of the arena through the Gate of Life. Before long the other gladiators finished their duels; forty-nine more winners and six of the losers who fought with enough heart to win their lives, courtesy of the emperor and the Roman people, took their turns basking in the glory of the crowd's attention.

Throughout the afternoon, more bloody battles were staged, each more bizarre than the last: twelve gladiators entered, each armed only with a trident and a dagger — no helmet and no shield — and climbed up a narrow ramp to a small wooden platform big enough for only one man. A heavily armored gladiator then attacked each platform using that same narrow ramp. Each attacking gladiator wore an elaborate helmet that completely covered his head and carried a large shield and a short stabbing sword. This deadly game of king of the hill was over when only one man remained standing on each platform.

Next a small army attacked, pillaged, and burned a fortress that was raised up from below the arena floor. After the carnage was cleared away, in rumbled eighty pairs of *essedarii* (chariot fighters). First they circled the arena amidst a choking cloud of dust. Then, suddenly, accompanied by bloodcurdling war cries, they wheeled around and made mad charges at each other across the sand, the drivers cracking their long whips at anything within their reach as their teammates hurled short javelins at their opponents. When the last chariot to remain upright rolled out of sight, in scurried the arena slaves to remove platforms, bodies, and bloody sand.

The crowd grew quiet, almost exhausted by the constant action in the arena. Sunset approached and the shadow of the great awning cut across the sand. Then, out of the shadow strutted six massive figures. When they stepped into the last rays of bright sunlight, their polished armor sparkled like the finest jewelry. The crowd gasped as one. They knew who these men were. They were the greatest gladiators in the whole Roman Empire. Urbico ("City Boy"), the *secutor*, was a twenty-two-year-old first-class fighter from Florence and had had thirteen victories. He would face Rapido, a *retiarius* known all over Rome for his lightning-fast reflexes. Felix ("Lucky") the *mirmillo,* a forty-five-year-old veteran from Gaul, would fight Aptus ("Ready") the Thracian, who was from Alexandria and the winner of thirty-seven combats. The last fight on the day's program, the main event, would feature the great Flamma ("Blaze" or "Flame"). He had not only won twenty-one times, but had won the *rudius*

66

an unprecedented four times. His opponent would be Generoso ("Noble" or "Well-born"), a handsome *retiarius* who was undefeated in twenty-seven fights. Generoso's flashy style and good looks made him the darling of the crowd, even if the huge, muscular Flamma was the bettors' favorite.

The stars of the show marched to the center of the arena and saluted the emperor. The crowd was on its feet, captivated. Three slaves entered the arena to display the victors' prizes, a silver bowl overflowing with gold coins and a palm branch symbolizing victory. The cheers of the crowd fell away to silence as Urbico and Rapido moved to the center of the arena and the other four champions disappeared under the stands. The two gladiators paused and raised their weapons in salute to each other. Then, in a flash, Urbico attacked. He threw himself at Rapido, hoping to knock him off balance and create an opening. But Urbico's every move was countered by Rapido's expert blocking with his trident. The fight moved back and forth across the amphitheater and the audience erupted with every thrust and parry. The audience knew that these two gladiators were perfectly matched. Sooner or later one fighter would tire and make a mistake. Gladiators this good never missed even the smallest opening in their enemy's defenses.

Then it happened: Rapido left his net on the ground a split second too long. Immediately Urbico trapped it under the bottom edge of his shield and lunged with his sword, striking Rapido under his left arm. Rapido dropped his trident and staggered back, his arm now useless. With no weapon and only one good arm Rapido couldn't possibly continue, so he raised his left index finger to ask for mercy. The emperor looked to the crowd for an answer. That answer came loud and clear: *"Mitte!"* Urbico bowed and accepted his winnings. In an exceptional display of camaraderie, he then helped his defeated foe out of the arena and to the infirmary deep inside the amphitheater. The audience, usually callous, was touched by Urbico's display of sportsmanship.

The second pair of champions entered: Felix, the well-known *mirmillo*, and Aptus, a Thracian with a nasty reputation. Fifty thousand pairs of eyes were riveted to the two gladiators below; no one dared blink, knowing that none of Aptus's thirty-seven fights lasted more than a minute. This one lasted ten seconds. Aptus used his small round shield as an offensive weapon and pounded Felix into the cold marble wall of the arena. With a flick of his wrist, the Thracian thrust his curved sword up under the *mirmillo's* helmet. Felix slid down the wall and keeled over in the sand, dead. As the arena slaves dragged Felix's body out through the Gate of Death, Aptus removed his helmet and blew kisses to the people of Rome.

All that remained of today's spectacle was the main event: Generoso versus Flamma, the most famous gladiator in the empire. From the moment it began, the spectators could tell that this duel could end in an upset. Flamma seemed slow; every time Generoso cast his net it would entangle the edge of the *secutor's* shield or the top of his helmet, and Flamma barely managed to escape. The sun dipped below the rim of the amphitheater as the two gladiators fought in the middle of the arena, circling each other and breathing hard. Flamma was wounded on his right shoulder, which slowed the thrusts of his sword. Generoso cast his net again and Flamma leapt to his left as the needle-sharp points of

Generoso's trident whistled past his face. Trying to gain the advantage, Flamma bashed into the net fighter with his shield. Generoso yanked back on his net, catching his opponent's heel, and sent him crashing to the sand. Flamma opened his eyes to see the trident poised above his throat. Generoso stood with one foot on Flamma's chest, now helpless on his back and at the mercy of the same crowd who had cheered his previous victories. Years of heroic service didn't matter to the mob, though. Flamma knew what the crowd wanted: his blood. But this time, because he had fought so well, or perhaps because they actually felt sympathy for this fallen hero, Flamma saw white handkerchiefs waving in the last rays of the Roman sun. And when he looked up to the imperial box, he saw the emperor turn his thumb up. Flamma thanked the gods, struggled to his feet, and limped through the Gate of Life, deciding at that moment to retire for good.

Generoso pranced around the arena, his arms raised in victory. A column of soldiers marched out to him and snapped to attention. An arena attendant walked through the line of soldiers to present him with the palm branch and the silver bowl filled with gold coins. He placed a laurel crown on his head and offered him the treasured *rudius,* the wooden baton that gave him freedom from the arena. The emperor stood and proclaimed Generoso the champion of the games. The crowd roared its approval as Generoso took his bows. The emperor waved to the audience one last time, then turned and led his entourage through his private tunnel back to the imperial palace. With this grand flourish the games ended, and the crowd made its way down the marble steps and out of the Colosseum. The darkening streets of Rome were filled

71

with their laughter and playful shouts; many were already making plans for the next show. As slaves pulled off his armor and massaged his aching muscles, Generoso was looking forward to a night of wild parties where he, the hero of the day, would be the guest of honor.

Note: There is no complete record of a day at the arena. This is a re-creation of what might have been presented in a typical imperial show in ancient Rome. It is a combination of events described in historical accounts and scenes from the amphitheater depicted in Roman artifacts. The wooden ship really did appear at the games of Emperor Septimus Severus in A.D. 202. The gladiators' names and records are real; they are taken from information engraved on their tombstones.

Urbico's tombstone

XI
THE END OF THE GLADIATORS

From the first recorded gladiator fights in 264 B.C. to their final abolition almost seven hundred years later, countless thousands died in the arena, all victims of some of the greatest exhibitions of brutality in history. The culture that produced the gladiators also created the atmosphere that eventually led to their extinction.

Like all great empires, Rome reached the height of its power and then, over a long period of time, began to collapse. It became impossible to maintain the huge armies needed to protect its borders from invaders, the vast numbers of people ruled by the empire became unmanageable, and the bureaucracy required to keep the government running became bloated and corrupt. The later emperors lacked the absolute power to demand the money and resources required to stage shows as extravagant as the ones given when Rome was at its apex.

Although Rome's glory faded over the centuries, Rome was still the major power of its time, and its subjects still expected to be amused by great shows. As time went on, novel acts were harder to create and exotic animals harder to obtain, and the shows became slightly less spectacular. The blood of innocent men and beasts continued to spill, however, and the crowds continued to enjoy the sight of pain and suffering.

It took the rise of a new faith to change the attitudes of ruler and ruled alike enough to stop gladiatorial combat. Christianity was born in the Roman Empire and found many converts among the poor and powerless. The pagan gods of Rome and the emperors who made themselves gods ruled the people with an attitude of total and merciless authority. These new Christians that preached peace and love often found themselves facing death in the arena when they refused to worship the emperor or his gods. The empire unknowingly aided the growth of this new faith. Every attempt to stop the spread of Christianity with the threat of persecution and death seemed to encourage more converts. These converts began to realize that the pain and terror inflicted in the arena was at odds with the gentle and merciful words of their new religion.

Christianity gained its most powerful convert in A.D. 312 when the emperor Constantine the Great adopted the faith and declared Christianity the state religion. He issued an edict abolishing gladiatorial combat in A.D. 323. This edict further stated that those condemned to the arena should serve their sentences in the mines instead. This was a humanitarian gesture in theory only, because forced labor in the mines was nearly as deadly as combat in the arena, though far less dramatic. This ban, however, was not enforced. Constantine himself allowed several gladiator shows to be given, contradicting his own law. It is proof of the

Gladiator shows continued in the reign of Constantine, the first Christian emperor.

powerful attraction of the games that even a great leader like Constantine could not or would not stop them completely. Crowds still filled amphitheaters all over the empire to watch gladiators do their bloody work. Christianity needed more time to wipe out all the pagan beliefs of Rome; even some of the gladiators were Christians. It wasn't until A.D. 367 that the emperor Valentinian I stopped the condemnation of Christians to the gladiator schools. Although emperor Honorius closed the gladiator schools in A.D. 399, the games still seemed to be thriving.

Five years later, a tragic event finally put an end to the gladiators. In A.D. 404, a Christian monk named Telemachus jumped into an arena in Rome and tried to separate two combatants. The crowd went berserk, climbed over the walls into the arena, and tore the monk limb from limb. In response to this ugly incident, the emperor Honorius immediately and permanently banned all gladiator combats. Unlike Constantine, he enforced the law.

The era of the gladiator was over. Though the Roman Empire was officially a Christian state for ninety-two years before gladiators were abolished, Christianity was primarily responsible for bringing an end to gladiator combats. Violence and cruelty would continue to be all too common in history, but never again would the amphitheater fill with people gathered to watch men kill each other for sport.

XII

THE INFLUENCE OF
THE GLADIATORS

While it has been 1,600 years since the last gladiator walked out of the arena, many elements of their games are alive and well. Around the world there are many buildings named after the structures used in ancient Rome for the gladiator shows. The Los Angeles Coliseum was built in 1932 for the summer Olympic games and was used again for the 1984 Olympic games. Today it is used for football games and can seat 100,000 people, twice as many as its Roman namesake. Buildings called arenas or amphitheaters are used for everything from tractor pulls to symphony concerts. In Spain, amphitheaters built by the Romans are still used for bullfights, which are the direct descendants of the animal fights of two thousand years ago.

Not only are the buildings patterned after Roman examples, but many sporting events are very similar to those seen in Roman times. Like the bullfights of Spain and Mexico, the rodeos of the United States and Canada include events any Roman would recognize. Bulldogging, an

77

opposite page: The monk Telemachus was killed by a mob of irate spectators after he tried to separate two fighting gladiators.

event in which a cowboy wrestles a bull to the ground by its horns, was introduced to Roman audiences by Julius Caesar. It then became known as Thessalonian bullfighting, since it originated in Thessaly (what is now Greece). The rodeo clowns that dash around the ring to distract the bulls and protect the cowboys use moves similar to those the *bestiarii* used to dodge the charges of the animals they fought. Modern horse racing in all its different forms is practiced throughout the world and features the same speed and excitement Romans enjoyed at chariot races. The careful breeding of horses and the heavy betting on races has changed very little over the centuries. The modern circus got its name from the chariot racing stadiums built all over the Roman Empire, and almost every circus act was perfected two thousand years before P. T. Barnum and the Ringling brothers were born. Trained lions and tigers, dancing elephants, acrobats, and jugglers had the same appeal then as they do now.

Gladiators no longer fight, but today's professional boxers and wrestlers use many of their techniques to win the crowd's attention. Wrestlers wear outrageous costumes and adopt flamboyant personalities. Boxers give themselves colorful nicknames to enhance their reputations and advertise their fighting prowess.

Modern athletes devote long hours to intense training and must have the same discipline and fierce competitive spirit that the gladiators had. For some, all the hard work pays off. The great sports stars of today are household names and make more money in one year than most people will see in their lifetimes. Champion gladiators enjoyed the same kind of fame, and the gold and prizes they won in the arena must have

opposite page: The descendants of the gladiator: the professional wrestler, the matador, the professional boxer, and the football player.

been as amazing to the average Roman as the multimillion-dollar contracts of today's pro athletes are to us.

There is really only one major difference between our modern sports and the games of the ancient gladiators: today's spectators no longer demand the blood of the participants. The competition is between winning and losing; for the gladiators it was between life and death.

Other Books of Interest

Burrell, Roy. *The Romans*. Oxford, England: Oxford University Press, 1991.

Clare, John D., Ed. *Classical Rome*. San Diego: Harcourt Brace, 1993.

Grant, Michael. *Gladiators*. New York: Delacorte Press, 1967.

James, Simon. *Ancient Rome*. New York: Alfred A. Knopf, 1990.

Pearson, John. *Arena: The Story of the Colosseum*. New York: McGraw-Hill, 1973.

Bibliography

Auguet, Roland. *Cruelty and Civilization: The Roman Games*. London: Allen and Unwin, 1972.

Balsdon, J. P. V. D. *Life and Leisure in Ancient Rome*. New York: McGraw-Hill, 1969.

Carcopino, J. *Daily Life in Ancient Rome*. New Haven, Conn.: Yale University Press, 1940.

Cozzo, Guiseppe. *Ingegneria Roma*. Rome: Multigrafica Editrice, 1970.

Friedlander, Ludwig. *Roman Life and Manners Under the Early Empire*. Translated by J. H. Freese, L. Magnus, and A. B. Gough. New York: E. P. Dutton, 1908.

Goldman, Norma. "Reconstructing the Roman Colosseum Awning." *Archaeology*, March/April 1982.

Grant, Michael. *Gladiators*. New York: Delacorte Press, 1967.

Hopkins, Keith. *Death and Renewal*. Cambridge: Cambridge University Press, 1983.

Jennison, George. *Animals for Show and Pleasure in Ancient Rome*. Manchester: Manchester University Press, 1937.

Lafaye, G. "Gladiateurs" in Daremberg, C. and Saglio, E. Vol. 2: 1563–99 of *Dictionnaire des Antiquites Greques et Romaines*. Paris: Hatchette, 1877–1919.

Pearson, John. *Arena: The Story of the Colosseum*. New York: McGraw-Hill, 1973.

Pflug, Hermann. *Antike Helme*. Koln: Rheinland-Verlag; Bonn: In Kommision bei R. Habett, 1989.

Robert, Louis. *Les Gladiatuers dans l'Orient grec*. Paris: E. Champion, 1940.

Sabbatini-Tumolesi, P., and Gregori, G. L. *Epigrafia anfiteatrale dell' Occidente Romano*. Rome: Quasar, 1988.

Glossary

arena the sand-covered fighting area in an amphitheater

amphitheater an oval-shaped building with a central fighting area surrounded by concentric rows of seats

auroch a large wild bison, now extinct

bestiarius an animal fighter

bireme a war galley with two tiers of oars on each side

bustiarius a gladiator who fought at a funeral

canistrum a spherical iron cage from inside which a bestiarius could safely confront wild animals in the arena

circus a chariot-racing stadium

Circus Maximus the largest chariot-racing stadium in Rome; it held more than 250,000 spectators

Colosseum the largest amphitheater in Rome, the Colosseum held 50,000 spectators; it was also called the *Amphitheatrum Flavium*

consul one of the two rulers of the Roman Republic, elected each year by the senate

damnati ad bestius to be sentenced to be killed by wild animals in the arena

damnati ad gladium to be sentenced to be executed by sword in the arena

damnati in ludum to be sentenced to a gladiator school and trained to fight in the arena

dimachaerus a gladiator who fought with a sword in each hand

editor the giver of the games, who decided if a defeated gladiator should live or die

eques a gladiator who fought on horseback with a round shield and a lance

essedarius a gladiator who fought in a horse-drawn chariot

fasces an ax surrounded by a bundle of rods; a symbol of Roman authority

forum a public square or marketplace; early gladiator displays often took place in Roman forums

galley an ancient warship propelled by oars

gladiator a professional swordsman who fought, usually to the death; gladiator combat was a form of popular entertainment in ancient Rome

gladiatores meridiani untrained slaves or criminals forced to execute one another

gladius a short, straight sword; the word *gladiator* is derived from this word

hoplomachus a heavily armored gladiator who wore a crested helmet and carried a long shield; replaced the earlier *Samnite* gladiator during the reign of Augustus

lacquearius a gladiator armed with a spear and a rope lasso to catch his opponent

lanista a businessman who organized gladiatorial displays for a fee

legionaries soldiers; a legion of the Roman army consisted of 3,000 to 6,000 men

lictor the traditional bodyguard of the consuls in the Roman republic; they carried the *fasces* at public ceremonies

ludi the Roman games: gladiator shows, wild animal fights, and chariot races; *ludus* also refers to a gladiator school

missilia numbered wooden balls thrown into the crowd during the games to be redeemed for prizes

missus to grant a defeated gladiator his life

munus a gladiator show

mirmillo a heavily armored gladiator often identified by the images of fish that decorated his helmet

naumachia a recreated sea battle that involved thousands of men

ocrea a metal leg guard

paegniarius a fighter who used a whip and a club against a similarly armed opponent; the paegniarius did not fight to the death and usually appeared at the beginning of a gladiator show

parma the small shield of a Thracian gladiator

patrician a Roman nobleman

plebeian a commoner in Roman society

podium in an amphitheater, the seating area closest to the arena; usually reserved for the nobility

pollice verso a thumbs-down gesture that served as a signal from the editor to kill a defeated gladiator

primus palus a first-class gladiator

quadrireme a war galley with four tiers of oars on each side

retiarius a gladiator who fought with a three-pronged spear and a net to catch his opponent

rudius a wooden baton given to a gladiator who had been granted retirement from combat; it was given only to the best and bravest gladiators

sagittarius an animal fighter armed with a bow and arrow

scutum a large, oblong shield

secutor a heavily armored gladiator; a *secutor* was always matched against a *retiarius*

sesterce a unit of Roman currency

sica the curved sword of the Thracian gladiator

spina the spine or divider in the middle of a chariot-racing track

tiro a novice gladiator

toga the formal robe of a Roman citizen

trident a three-pronged fishing spear

trireme a war galley with three tiers of oars on each side

tuba a Roman war trumpet

velarium an awning suspended by ropes over an amphitheater to protect the spectators from the sun

venabulum a long-bladed spear

venatio a show that often featured trained animals performing tricks, wild animal hunts, animals fighting each other, and animals killing condemned criminals

Index